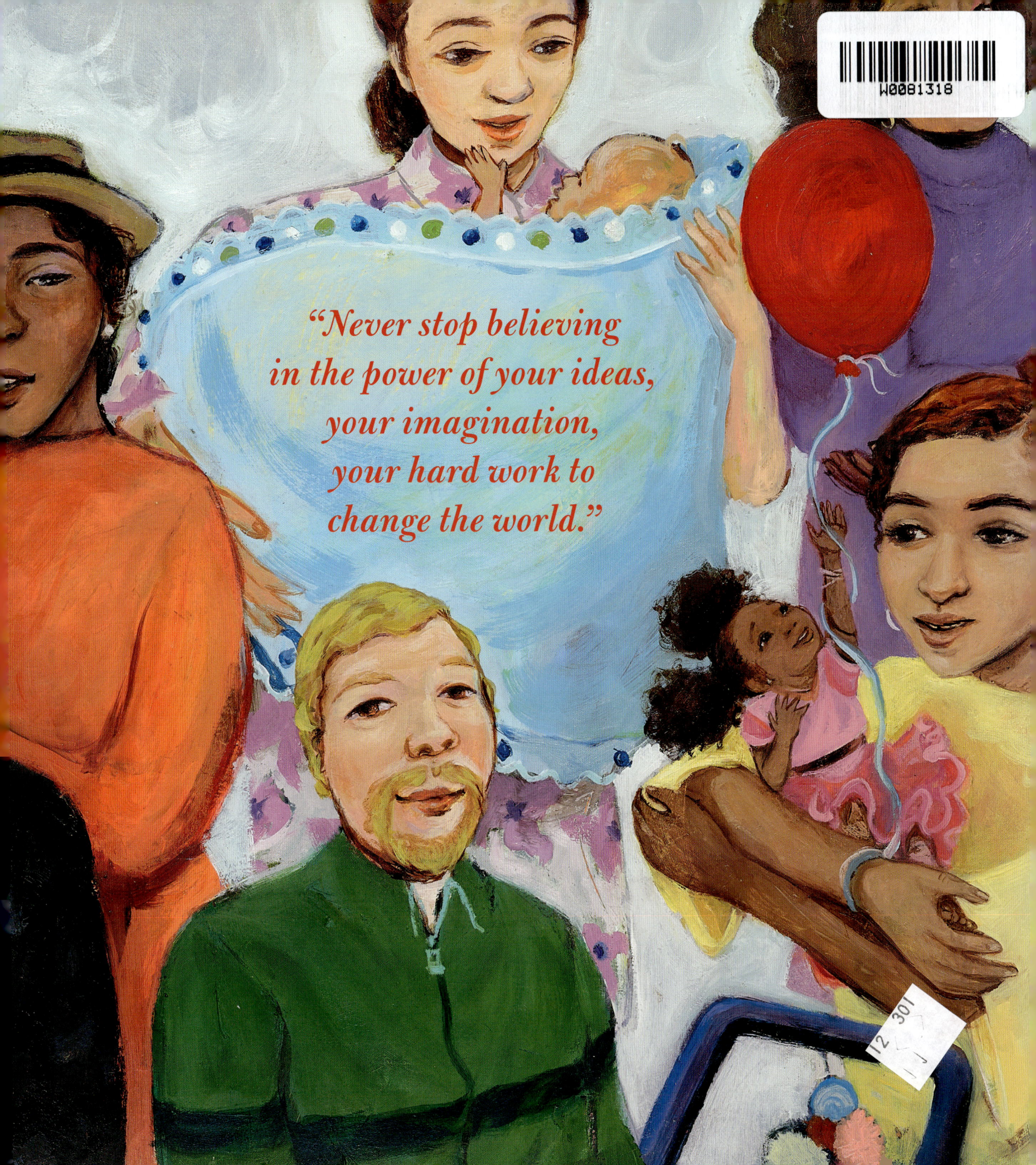

"*Never stop believing
in the power of your ideas,
your imagination,
your hard work to
change the world.*"

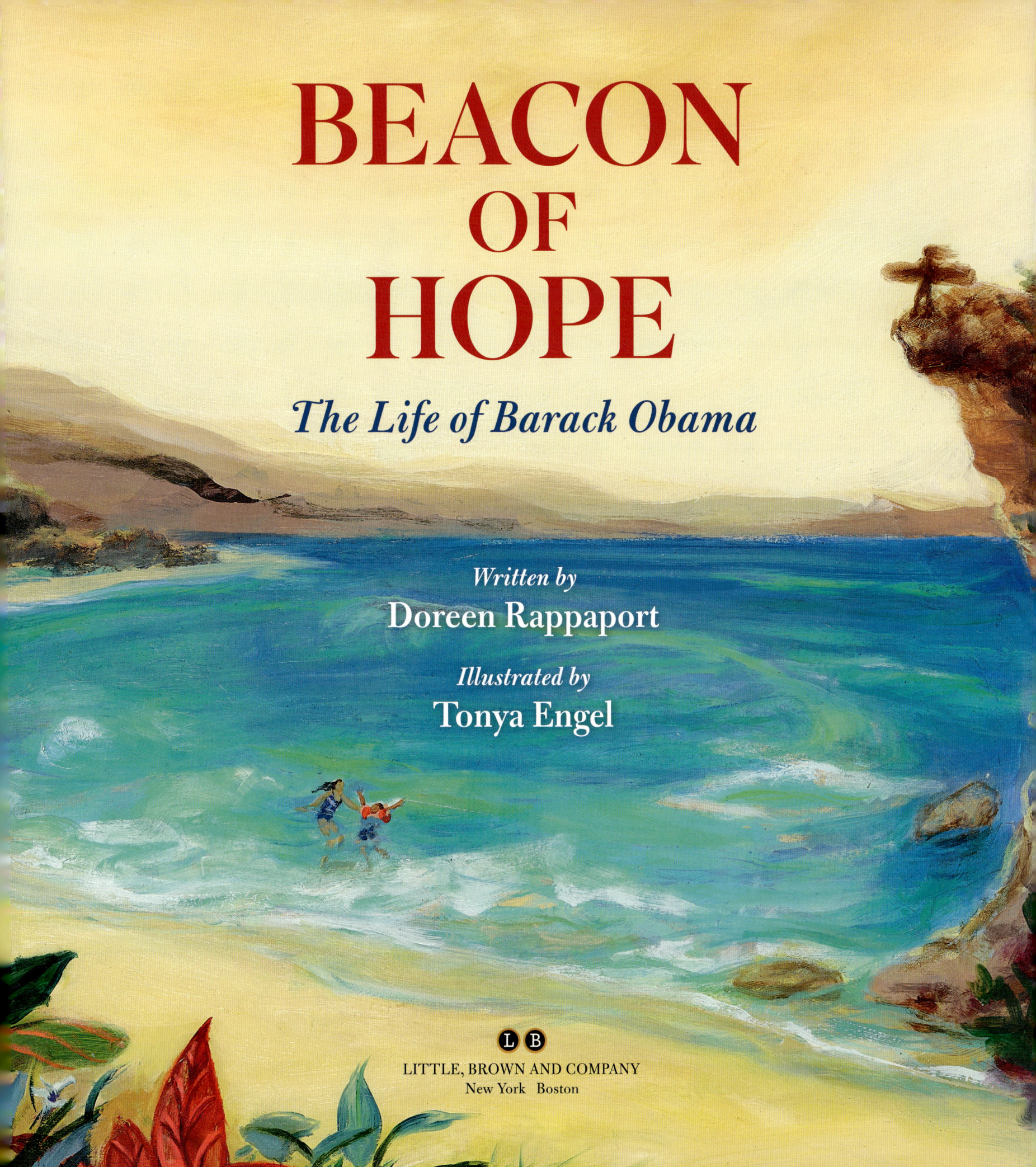

BEACON
OF
HOPE

The Life of Barack Obama

Written by
Doreen Rappaport

Illustrated by
Tonya Engel

L B
LITTLE, BROWN AND COMPANY
New York Boston

Ginger blossoms scenting the warm air.
Surfers gliding on ocean waves.
Runners jogging on Kailua Beach.
Hikers climbing through rainforests.
August 4, 1961, was a typical day
on Oahu, a Hawaiian island that
many people call a paradise.

But for Kansas-born Ann Dunham
and Kenyan-born Barack Obama Sr.,
August 4 was a special day:
It marked the birth of their son, Barack Jr.,
whom everyone called Barry or Ber.

Unfortunately, their marriage faltered,
and they separated shortly after Barry's birth.
Barack Sr. eventually returned to Kenya.
Ann completed college in Hawaii.
In 1965, she married Lolo Soetoro, and
she and Barry moved to Indonesia, Lolo's country.

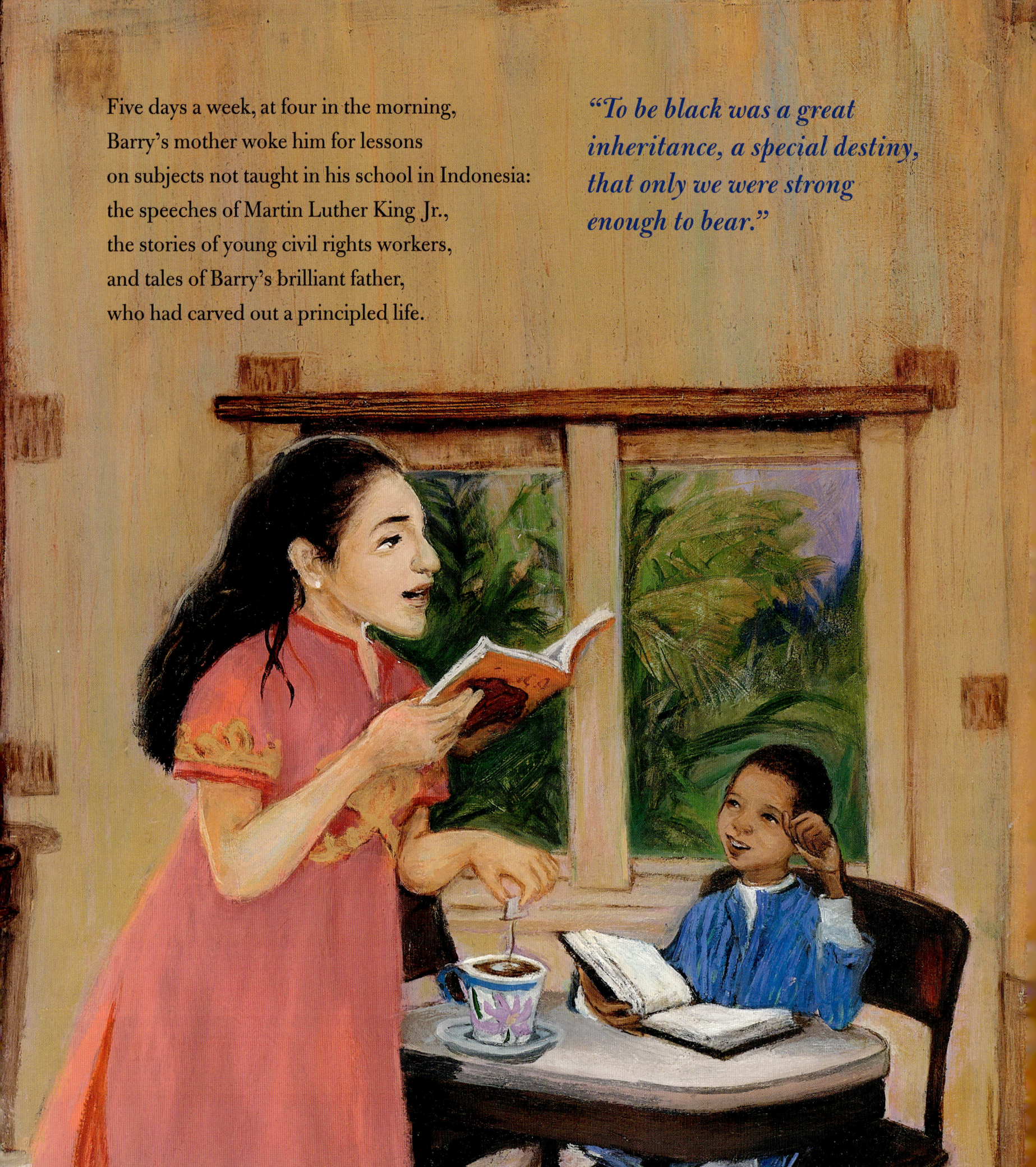

Five days a week, at four in the morning,
Barry's mother woke him for lessons
on subjects not taught in his school in Indonesia:
the speeches of Martin Luther King Jr.,
the stories of young civil rights workers,
and tales of Barry's brilliant father,
who had carved out a principled life.

*"To be black was a great
inheritance, a special destiny,
that only we were strong
enough to bear."*

Barry's kind, patient stepfather, Lolo,
who never raised his voice,
introduced Barry to people as his son.
He created a backyard mini zoo
with ducks, chickens, roosters, cockatoos,
two baby crocodiles, and an ape named Tata,
which Barry loved.

Many other people in Indonesia,
living in hovels, were not as lucky.

*"I saw extreme poverty at
a very early age. It left a
very strong mark on me."*

When Barry was nine, his sister Maya was born.
He loved her and his life in Indonesia,
but his mother believed he would get
a better education in the United States.
She sent him to Hawaii to live with her parents.
She and Maya stayed in Indonesia with Lolo.

Barry found a warm, loving home
with Gramps and Toot, who doted on him.
He joined the surfers and hikers and
runners and sand-castle-builders in Oahu.

School proved more of a challenge.
Oahu had many people of Asian
and Pacific Islander descent
but few Black Americans.
When Barry's teacher introduced him
as *Barack*, kids laughed at his unfamiliar name.
"Can I touch your hair?"
"Does your father eat people?"

Only one other Black student in his grade.
Only four among 3,622 children in the school.

*"The novelty of having me in the class
quickly wore off, but my sense
that I didn't belong continued to grow."*

When Barry was nine, his father came back
to Oahu for a monthlong visit.
Barry had only seen his father in photographs.
He looked so much smaller in person.

His father's deep, rich voice
telling stories captivated Barry,
but his constant advice about
what Barry should or should not do
grated on him.

*"He always felt he was right
about everything."*

There were times of tenderness, though.
Afternoons they read silently together.
His father shared his love of jazz
and the joy of dancing.
He gifted Barry his first basketball.
The sport became Barry's passion
for the rest of his life.

*"I grew accustomed to
his company. But then,
he was gone, and I never
saw him again."*

In high school, Barry began to feel
even more confused about his racial identity.
Few people in Oahu looked like him.

*"Growing up, I wasn't always
sure who I was."*

His loving grandparents and mother
could not offer guidance.
He shared his confusions
with a few Black friends, but
there were no Black adults around
who helped him sort out his feelings.
Occasional letters from his father,
living 10,000 miles away in Kenya,
offered no comfort.
Barry stopped writing back.

On his own, Barry explored Black history and culture.
The courageous civil rights workers inspired him.
Writers James Baldwin and Langston Hughes
and Black Nationalist leader Malcolm X
wrote about the struggle of being Black in America.

In college, Barry gradually began using his birth name, Barack, the same name as his father. His studies in California brought more talk with friends about race and injustice and inequality.

In his junior year, he transferred to Columbia University in New York.

"I wanted to be around more black folks in big cities."

He buckled down to studying, reading, and thinking about what would give his life purpose.

"I had a hunger to make the world a better place."

After graduation, he moved to Chicago to be a community organizer, to be like the civil rights activists who had worked with Black Southerners to end segregation.

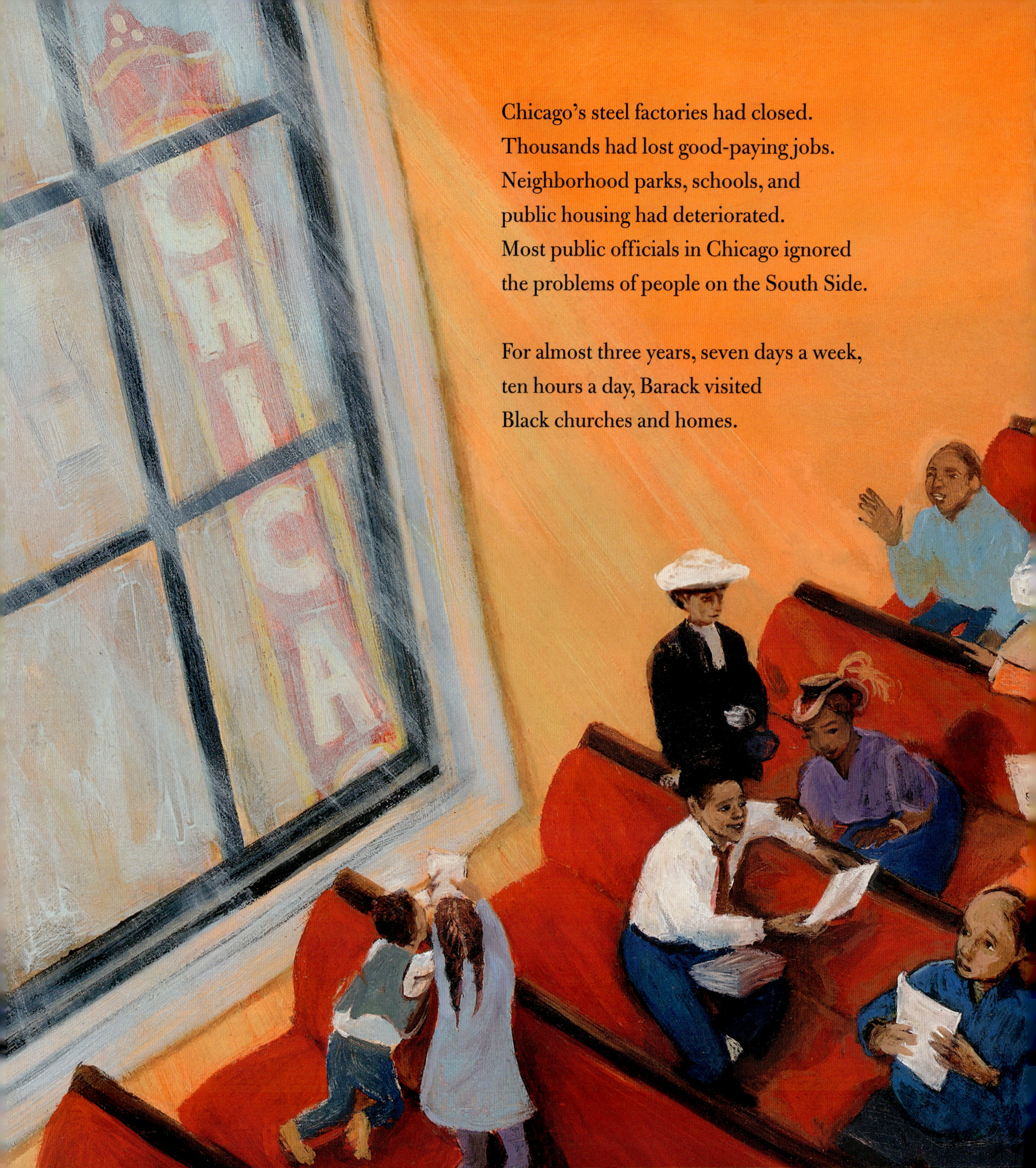

Chicago's steel factories had closed.
Thousands had lost good-paying jobs.
Neighborhood parks, schools, and
public housing had deteriorated.
Most public officials in Chicago ignored
the problems of people on the South Side.

For almost three years, seven days a week,
ten hours a day, Barack visited
Black churches and homes.

People shared their lives, and he shared his.
He listened and learned what they needed
to better their world.
He trained community leaders to pressure
public officials to make changes.

*"I came to love the men and women
I worked with."*

In church, he experienced how faith
offered people strength and courage.
For the first time in twenty-four years,
he felt part of a community.

"I came home in Chicago."

Auma, Barack's sister from their father's
first marriage, visited him in Chicago.
From the instant they hugged,
he loved her.
Auma shared her life with their father,
who had died almost three years before.
Sadly, their father's early bright future had ended
in bitterness and defeat.

*"I felt as if my world had been
turned on its head."*

His father had been his role model,
even though they had stopped communicating.
Now who did he have to guide him?
Auma encouraged Barack to visit Kenya
to better understand the world that had
shaped their father. And he did.

Five weeks of family gatherings.
Meeting his grandmother,
his father's two other wives,
his five brothers, aunts, and great-aunts.
The meals, the give-and-take, the talk.
Similar to so many evenings in Chicago.

He began to understand his father's struggles,
and his own struggles became clearer.

"The pain I felt was my father's pain.
My questions were my brothers' questions.
Their struggle, my birthright."

Organizing in Chicago brought small victories,
but no matter how hard Barack worked,
so many things could not be changed
on the local level.
Perhaps the law held answers.

*"I had things to learn
in law school that would help
bring about real change."*

Barack's election as the first Black president of the *Harvard Law Review* garnered attention all over the world. Upon his graduation, prestigious job offers poured in. He chose to return to Chicago, where he practiced civil rights law, taught at Chicago Law School, and led the Illinois chapter of Project Vote— registering 111,000 new Democratic Party voters.

Chicago was also where he found his life partner.

Michelle Robinson's family was rooted
in Chicago's South Side.
Dinner every night was a family affair.
Aunts, uncles, cousins often dropping by.
Money was not plentiful, but love was.
Education was foremost.
Michelle and her brother, Craig,
had attended Princeton University.
Michelle had gone on to Harvard Law.

Barack's and Michelle's family lives
sharply contrasted but shared
the same values of hard work,
education, and racial equality.

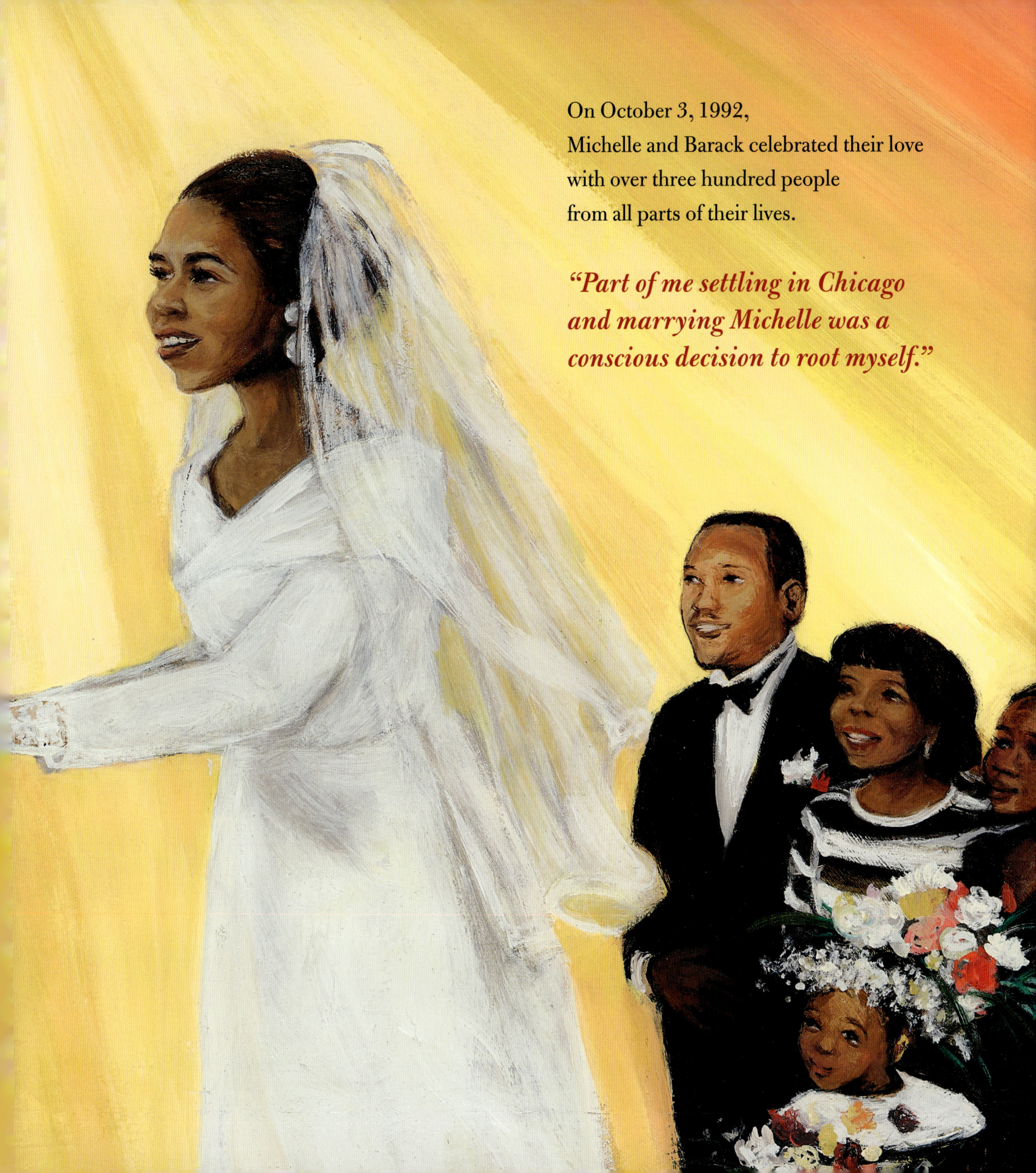

On October 3, 1992,
Michelle and Barack celebrated their love
with over three hundred people
from all parts of their lives.

*"Part of me settling in Chicago
and marrying Michelle was a
conscious decision to root myself."*

Barack believed elected officials
held the power to better people's lives.
For almost eight years, he served as a
Democratic state senator in Illinois,
working well with Republicans.
But he was restless and ambitious.
So many problems could not be solved
at the state level.

He ran for the US House of Representatives
and was beaten badly in the Democratic primary.
He decided to run for the US Senate next.

*"If I did win, I could have
a big impact."*

Reporters constantly questioned him
if his race and foreign-sounding name
might make people hesitate to vote for him.

*"I have an unusual name
and exotic background,
but my values are
essential American values."*

On the road for two years, away from Michelle
and his two young daughters, Malia and Sasha,
campaigning all over Illinois.
Barack spoke up for universal health care
and against invading the country of Iraq.

Americans were sharply divided over
how to make the country better.
Barack tackled this disunity in a speech
at the Democratic National Convention.

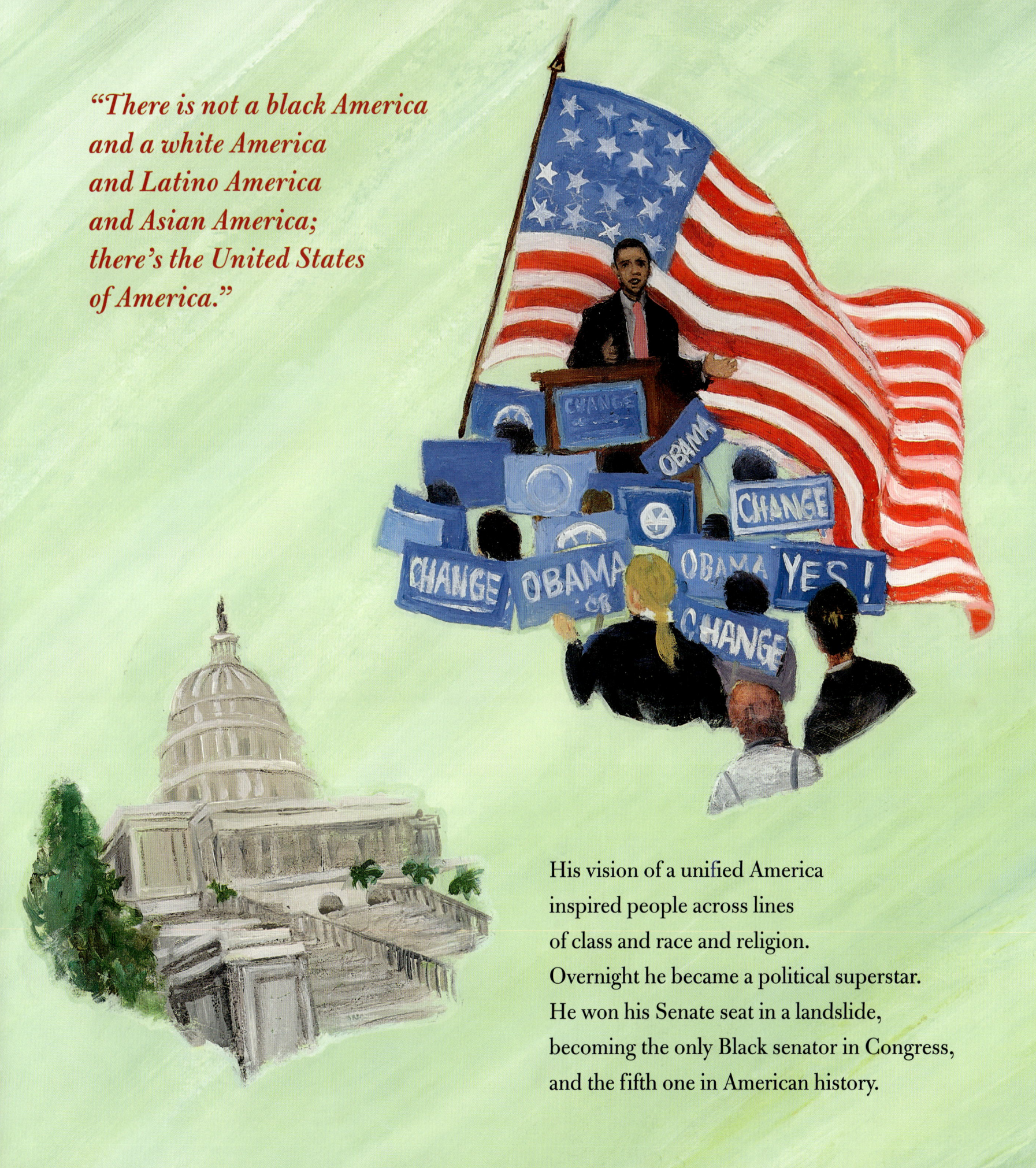

"There is not a black America and a white America and Latino America and Asian America; there's the United States of America."

His vision of a unified America
inspired people across lines
of class and race and religion.
Overnight he became a political superstar.
He won his Senate seat in a landslide,
becoming the only Black senator in Congress,
and the fifth one in American history.

Two years later, Barack was restless again.
He believed the Republican president
and Republican Congress were failing
to help most Americans.
He decided to run for president.

Again the question:
Would America's long history of racism
make many white Americans unwilling
to vote for a Black president?

"I believe America is ready."

Twenty-one more months away from his family.
He won a hard-fought Democratic primary
against Hillary Clinton,
an opponent of great accomplishment,
then won the presidency with
his message of hope and change.

*"They say we can't change
Washington. I say,
'Yes we can.'"*

On January 20, 2009, 1.8 million people
stood in the bitter cold to celebrate the
inauguration of America's first Black president.

Most of the country and the world
greeted the new president
with hope and enthusiasm.
He circled the globe, cementing ties
with allies and seeking new ones.
He helped negotiate a treaty of 198 nations
to reduce greenhouse gas emissions.
A deal with Iran stopped their production
of nuclear weapons.
A treaty with Russia reduced their
arsenal of nuclear warheads.

He won the Nobel Peace Prize
for his efforts at cooperation
between peoples all over the world
and for his vision to eliminate
nuclear weapons.

*"Only a just peace based
on the inherent rights and
dignity of every individual
can truly be lasting."*

Daily life in Washington was
a whirlwind of meetings with
lawmakers, cabinet members,
military leaders, diplomats,
and heads of agencies.

Early evenings were a joyous oasis.
Sasha and Malia campaigning for a family dog
and chattering away about new friends.
Michelle explaining Let's Move!, her project
encouraging healthy habits for children.
And Grandma Marian, joining the fun
and helping when needed.

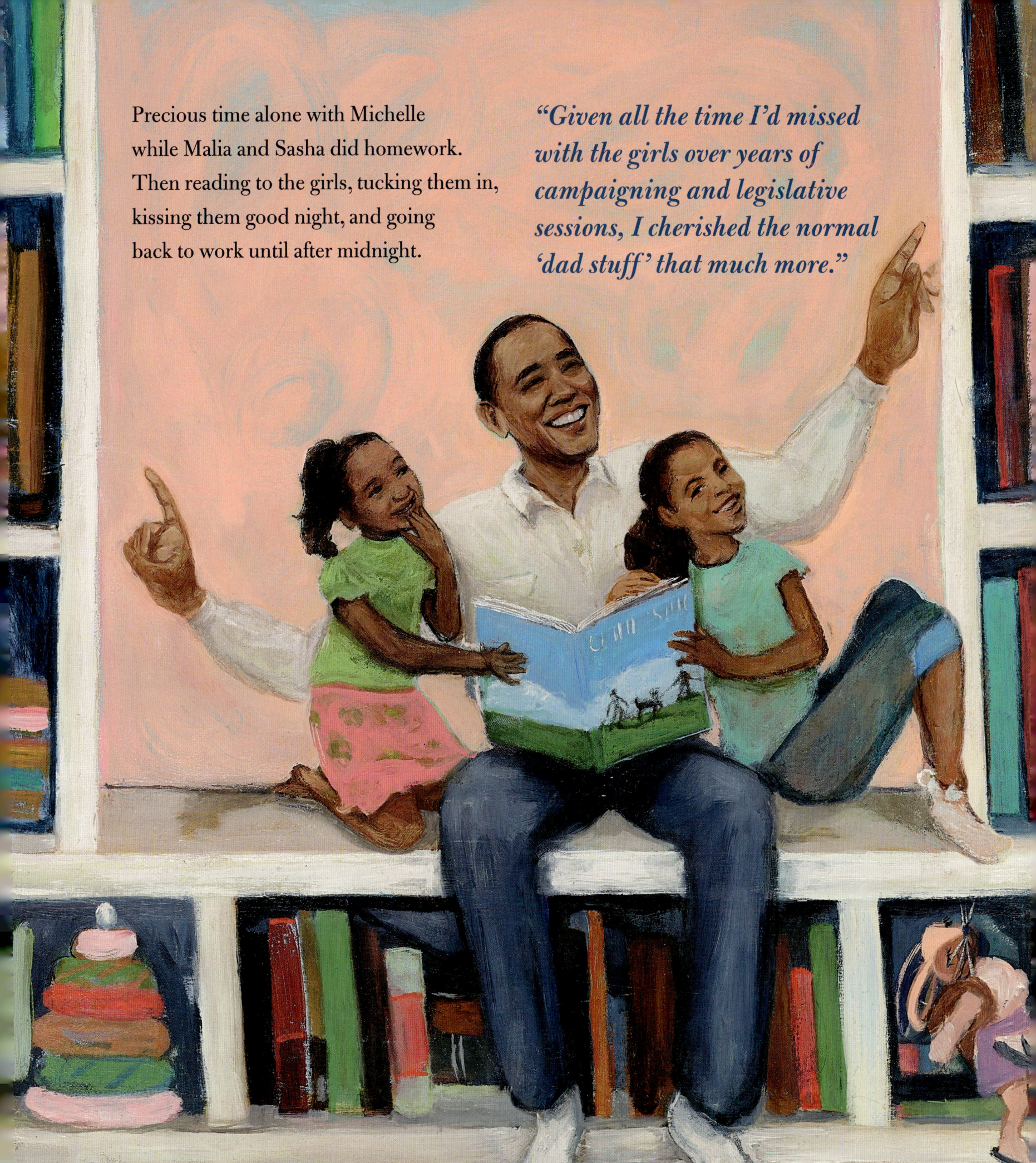

Precious time alone with Michelle while Malia and Sasha did homework. Then reading to the girls, tucking them in, kissing them good night, and going back to work until after midnight.

"Given all the time I'd missed with the girls over years of campaigning and legislative sessions, I cherished the normal 'dad stuff' that much more."

The country was in an economic crisis.

Businesses were closing.

Banks were near collapse.

Each month saw 700,000 lost jobs.

Barack held meeting after meeting,

questioning and listening to experts,

and created a plan to rescue the economy.

Americans began to feel more confident.

On to the next challenge.

Nearly fifty million Americans had no health insurance.

Many sick people didn't go to doctors

because they didn't have money

to pay them or to buy medicine.

"In the wealthiest nation on Earth, no one should go broke just because they get sick."

Again, Barack met with experts
to create a medical insurance plan
that Americans could afford.
The Affordable Care Act covered
even Americans who were already sick.
Twenty million people who had
never had health coverage now had it.

Republicans opposed almost all of Barack's ideas
and voted against almost all of his programs.
Racist attacks and lies on the
radio, television, and Internet
convinced millions of Americans that
Barack was not born in the United States
and was ineligible to be the president.
Many of Barack's supporters were disappointed
that he did not counter the vicious assaults,
choosing instead to ignore the taunts and forge ahead.

He ended the war in Iraq and significantly
reduced the number of troops in Afghanistan.
He sent Special Forces to kill Osama Bin Laden,
the Al-Qaeda leader responsible for
the September 11, 2001, attacks
that killed 2,997 people.

"On nights like this one, we can say to those families who have lost loved ones to Al-Qaeda's terror: Justice has been done."

Barack believed America's greatest strength
was the diversity of its people.
More women and people of color were hired
to work for his administration.
He nominated Sonia Sotomayor as
the first Latinx Supreme Court Justice
and nominated Elena Kagan to be
the fourth woman justice.
He supported same-sex marriage and
the rights of LGBTQ Americans to serve
in the country's armed forces.
He issued executive orders that
didn't require Republican support.

"Where they won't act, I will."

One executive order protected 800,000
undocumented young adults, who were brought
into the country when they were children,
from being deported.

Barack's accomplishments were many, and
he never lost faith that a divided America
could be united.

*"I am the eternal optimist. I think that
over time people respond to civility
and rational arguments."*

AUTHOR'S NOTE

Writing a biography is a big responsibility. The first step is research to secure the facts of a person's life. Next, to assure that the facts are accurate, writers compare the information in different sources. Writers then use these facts to develop their own theme or interpretation of a person's life.

I see President Obama's life as a series of journeys—geographical, educational, and emotional. Each one brought new problems to solve, and new thoughts and feelings as he grappled with his racial identity and how he could give meaning to his life. His journeys took him to many places: Hawaii; Indonesia; California; New York City; Chicago; Kenya; Cambridge, Massachusetts; and Washington, DC. The warmth of sunny Hawaii and California and their laid-back lifestyles sharply contrasted with the immensity and intensity of life in New York City and Chicago. His trip to Kenya connected him with his father's family and his ancestry. His time at Harvard Law School sharply contrasted with the reality of life on the South Side of Chicago, which eventually propelled him to seek the presidency.

Writing about President Obama's life led me to examine my own journeys as I worked over the years to shape a legacy I could be proud of. I saw the connections from one time in my life to another time to another time. You will embark on many journeys of your own.

ILLUSTRATOR'S NOTE

As an illustrator, my role is instrumental in telling a story—I am like a griot weaving together histories and settings and timelines using colors, ideas, expressions, and movement. Research and accuracy are very important in a biography, but so is the relaying of a character's feelings, purpose, drive, and impact on the world around them. Taking time to examine President Obama's life became a whole new way of appreciating him and his family and revisiting this era in our history. I also found such joy in revisiting the power of Obama's presence—his direct impact on any room that he entered from the time that he was a child, to his presidency, to the present. Like the author of this book, I couldn't help but reflect on how his life, his journey, and the branches that join his, mine, and our ancestors' lives are exactly what legacies are meant to embody.

I begin each page as a drawing that gets transferred to heavyweight Bristol vellum paper, then use that surface to underpaint textures using acrylics. Afterward I complete the layering using oils and transparent glazes.

IMPORTANT EVENTS

February 2, 1961: Barack Hussein Obama Sr. and Stanley Ann Dunham marry.

August 4, 1961: Barack Hussein Obama Jr. is born in Honolulu, Hawaii, to Barack Obama Sr. and Stanley Ann Dunham.

January 1964: Ann files for divorce.

March 15, 1965: Stanley Ann Dunham marries Lolo Soetoro.

1967: Ann and Barack join Lolo in Indonesia.

August 15, 1970: Maya Soetoro is born.

1971–1979: Barack attends Punahou School in Honolulu.

1979–1983: For two years, Barack attends Occidental College in Los Angeles, California, then transfers to Columbia University in New York City.

July 29, 1985–May 1988: Barack works as a community organizer in Chicago.

Summer 1988: Barack travels to Kenya to meet his paternal family.

1988–1991: Barack attends Harvard Law School.

October 3, 1992: Michelle LaVaughn Robinson and Barack Hussein Obama marry.

April–October 1992: Barack heads Illinois Project Vote.

1992–2004: He teaches at the University of Chicago Law School.

1993–2004: He works at the law firm Davis, Miner, Barnhill & Galland.

September 1995: Barack's book *Dreams from My Father* is published.

January 8, 1997–November 4, 2003: He serves as an Illinois state senator.

July 4, 1998: Malia Ann Obama is born.

March 21, 2000: Barack loses the Democratic primary for the US House of Representatives to Bobby Rush.

June 10, 2001: Natasha (Sasha) Marian Obama is born.

March 16, 2004: Barack wins the Democratic primary for US Senate.

July 27, 2004: Barack gives the keynote speech at the Democratic National Convention.

January 4, 2005–2008: Barack serves as an Illinois senator in the US Senate.

October 2006: Barack's second book, *The Audacity of Hope*, is published.

February 10, 2007: Barack announces his campaign for the presidency.

November 4, 2008: Barack Obama is elected president with nearly 53 percent of the popular vote and 365 electoral votes. Joseph Biden becomes the vice president elect.

January 20, 2009: Barack is inaugurated as the forty-fourth president of the United States.

February 17, 2009: The American Recovery and Reinvestment Act becomes law.

August 8, 2009: Sonia Sotomayor is sworn in to the US Supreme Court, becoming its first woman of color, first Latinx person, and first Latina member.

October 9, 2009: Barack Obama is awarded the Nobel Peace Prize.

March 23, 2010: The Patient Protection and Affordable Care Act becomes law.

April 8, 2010: The New Strategic Arms Reduction Treaty (START) is signed, reducing the stockpile of nuclear weapons in Russia and in the United States.

July 21, 2010: The Dodd-Frank Wall Street Reform and Consumer Protection Act passes.

August 7, 2010: Elena Kagan is sworn in to the US Supreme Court.

December 13, 2010: The Healthy, Hunger-Free Kids Act, an outgrowth of Michelle Obama's Let's Move! program, funds nutritional and free lunch programs.

December 22, 2010: President Obama repeals the Don't Ask, Don't Tell policy, allowing gay, lesbian, and bisexual people to openly serve in the US Armed Forces.

May 1, 2011: He announces the death of Osama Bin Laden.

May 9, 2012: He announces his support of same-sex marriage.

November 6, 2012: President Obama is reelected.

January 21, 2013: President Obama is inaugurated for the second time.

July 21, 2014: An executive order protects the rights of LGBTQ employees in the workforce.

June 26, 2015: The US Supreme Court rules 5–4 that the Constitution guarantees a right to same-sex marriage.

August 3, 2015: The Clean Power Plan sets the goal of reducing carbon pollution from power plants by more than 30 percent by 2030.

January 17, 2016: The Joint Comprehensive Plan of Action preventing Iran from acquiring nuclear weapons is finalized.

January 20, 2017: President Obama's two terms officially end.

SELECTED BIBLIOGRAPHY

Alter, Jonathan. *The Promise: President Obama, Year One*. New York: Simon & Schuster, 2010.

—*The Center Holds: Obama and His Enemies*. New York: Simon & Schuster, 2013.

Baker, Peter. *Obama: The Call of History*. New York: Callaway, 2017.

Finnegan, William. "The Candidate: How the Son of a Kenyan Economist Became an Illinois Everyman." *New Yorker*, May 31, 2004.

Garrow, David. *Rising Star: The Making of Barack Obama*. New York: William Morrow, 2017.

Harnden, Toby. "Barack Obama's True Colours: The Making of the Man Who Would Be US President." *Telegraph*, 2008.

MacFarquhar, Larissa. "The Conciliator: Where Is Barack Obama Coming From?" *New Yorker*, April 30, 2007.

Mendell, David. *Obama: From Promise to Power*. New York: Amistad, 2007.

Obama, Auma. *And Then Life Happens: A Memoir*. Translated by Ross Benjamin. New York: St. Martin's Press, 2012.

Obama, Barack. *A Promised Land*. New York: Crown, 2020.

—*Dreams from My Father. A Story of Race and Inheritance*. New York: Crown, 1995.

—*The Audacity of Hope: Thoughts on Reclaiming the American Dream*. New York: Crown, 2006.

Obama, Michelle. *Becoming*. New York: Crown, 2018.

Obama White House Archives. obamawhitehouse.archives.gov.

Plouffe, David. *The Audacity to Win*. New York: Viking, 2009.

Remnick, David. *The Bridge: The Life and Rise of Barack Obama*. New York: Alfred A. Knopf, 2010.

SOURCE NOTES

In many instances, quotes by Barack Obama have been shortened without changing their meaning, and punctuation has been simplified. The text begins on page 7. The quotes on pages 8, 11, 13, 21, and 22 are from *Dreams from My Father*. The quotes on pages 9 and 12 are from *Rising Star*. The quote on page 14 is from remarks made in Mt. Vernon, Iowa, "A Call to Serve," on December 5, 2007. The quotes on pages 16, 17, 20, 30, 31, and the second quote on page 27 are from *The Bridge*. The first quote on page 19, the first quote on page 27, and the quote on page 35 are from *A Promised Land*. The second quote on page 19 is from an interview with *Hyde Park Herald*. The quote on page 25 is from "Barack Obama's True Colours." The quote on page 29 is from a speech at the Democratic National Convention on July 27, 2004. The quote on page 32 is from remarks at the acceptance of the Nobel Peace Prize on December 10, 2009. The quote on page 36 is from remarks at Prince George's Community College on September 26, 2013. The quote on page 39 is from a statement made on May 1, 2011. The first quote on page 41 is from a speech in Las Vegas, Nevada, on October 24, 2011. The second quote on page 41 is from President Obama's first prime-time televised news conference in the White House on February 9, 2009. The quote on the front endpapers is from remarks at the White House Science Fair on March 23, 2015. The quote on the back endpapers is from a speech made on February 5, 2008.

For Burnell Eubanks, Thelma Eubanks, Freddie Green, Karen Pate, Mr. Holmes
—DR

Dedicated to my mother, Sherry, who was fifteen years old in 1965
when southern Black people could finally and freely
exercise their voting rights (with the Voting Rights Act).
—TE

About This Book

The illustrations for this book were done in oil glazes over acrylic medium on heavy vellum paper. This book was edited by Deirdre Jones and designed by Patrick Collins with art direction by Saho Fujii. The production was supervised by Patricia Alvarado, and the production editor was Annie McDonnell. The text was set in Bulmer MT Standard, and the display type is Superior Title.

Text copyright © 2025 by Doreen Rappaport • Illustrations copyright © 2025 by Tonya Engel • Cover illustration copyright © 2025 by Tonya Engel. Cover design by Patrick Collins • Cover copyright © 2025 by Hachette Book Group, Inc. • Hachette Book Group supports the right to free expression and the value of copyright. The purpose of copyright is to encourage writers and artists to produce the creative works that enrich our culture. • The scanning, uploading, and distribution of this book without permission is a theft of the author's intellectual property. If you would like permission to use material from the book (other than for review purposes), please contact permissions@hbgusa.com. Thank you for your support of the author's rights. • Little, Brown and Company • Hachette Book Group • 1290 Avenue of the Americas, New York, NY 10104 • Visit us at LBYR.com • First Edition: January 2025 • Little, Brown and Company is a division of Hachette Book Group, Inc. • The Little, Brown name and logo are registered trademarks of Hachette Book Group, Inc. • The publisher is not responsible for websites (or their content) that are not owned by the publisher. • Little, Brown and Company books may be purchased in bulk for business, educational, or promotional use. For information, please contact your local bookseller or the Hachette Book Group Special Markets Department at special.markets@hbgusa.com. • Library of Congress Cataloging-in-Publication Data • Names: Rappaport, Doreen, author. | Engel, Tonya, illustrator. • Title: Beacon of hope: the life of Barack Obama / written by Doreen Rappaport ; illustrated by Tonya Engel. • Other titles: Life of Barack Obama • Description: First edition. | New York : Little, Brown and Company, 2025. | Series: A big words book | Includes bibliographical references. | Audience: Ages 4–8 | Summary: "A biography of President Barack Obama." —Provided by publisher. • Identifiers: LCCN 2023059548 | ISBN 9780316397834 (hardcover) • Subjects: LCSH: Obama, Barack—Juvenile literature. | Presidents—United States—Biography—Juvenile literature. | African American politicians—Biography—Juvenile literature. | Politicians—United States—Biography—Juvenile literature. | United States—Politics and government—2009–2017—Juvenile literature. • Classification: LCC E908 .R37 2025 | DDC 973.932092 [B]—dc23/eng/20240108 • LC record available at https://lccn.loc.gov/2023059548 • ISBN 978-0-316-39783-4 • PRINTED IN DONGGUAN, CHINA • APS • 10 9 8 7 6 5 4 3 2 1

"Change will not come if we wait for some other person or if we wait for some other time. We are the ones we've been waiting for. We are the change that we seek."